"You can motivate them. You can direct their energies. You can teach them, lead them, and guide them. But you can't control them— and you wouldn't want to if you could."

"Real coaching takes place one player at a time. Forget those fiery 'Win one for the Gipper!' locker room speeches (or the business equivalent, the 'motivational meeting'). That's not where the coaching really happens. You'll do your most effective coaching one-on-one, face-to-face—without ever raising your voice."

How to Be a Great Coach

✓ 24 Lessons for Turning on the Productivity of Every Employee

MARSHALL J. COOK

New York Chicago San Francisco Lisbon
London Madrid Mexico City Milan New Delhi
San Juan Seoul Singapore Sydney Toronto

ISBN: 978-0-07-159136-2
MHID: 0-07-159136-2

This publication is designed to provide accurate and authorita-
tive information in regard to the subject matter covered. It is
sold with the understanding that the publisher is not engaged
in rendering legal, accounting, or other professional service. If
legal advice or other expert assistance is required, the services
of a competent professional person should be sought.
—*From a Declaration of Principles Jointly Adopted by a
Committee of the American Bar Association and a
Committee of Publishers and Associations*

McGraw-Hill books are available at special quantity discounts
to use as premiums and sales promotions, or for use in corpo-
rate training programs. To contact a representative, please visit
the Contact Us pages at www.mhprofessional.com.

This book is printed on acid-free paper.

Contents

☑ How to be a great coach

Each of the 24 lessons in this guide will take you only a few minutes to read, but they'll serve you well throughout your managerial career. They'll help you become an effective coach.

That's right. We didn't say "boss" or "supervisor." These days, the effective manager reaches their goals by coaching employees to peak performance.

In these simple lessons, you learn the techniques for good one-on-one coaching, and you learn why coaching is the most effective way to improve your employees' productivity and attitudes.

You'll understand the three natural motivations that drive any worker—including you—and learn how to focus those motivations on the job at hand.

You discover why you should talk less and listen more, issue challenges instead of orders, and prevent problems, rather than waiting to try to fix them.

You'll practice the art of asking good questions—and really hearing the answers—to get valuable input from the people closest to the job while boosting worker morale.

You encounter techniques for problem solving with your workers, empowering them to make decisions without losing your authority.

And, when it comes time for you to make the tough call, this guide outlines a decision-making process and reveals the three things you don't have to be to make a good decision.

If that decision involves delivering bad news to your employees, we can help you do that well, too.

Most employees think of memos and meetings as bad news, and we offer strategies for keeping these to a minimum. But we also show you how to craft effective memos and chair good meetings (yes, there is such a thing!).

You learn three of the most-important management concepts ever: how to reward what you want, how to provide effective feedback, and how to advocate for your employees with upper management.

As you learn to be a better coach, you'll develop willing colleagues, rather than compliant slaves. Your employees will own the process, take responsibility for their work, and share in the pride of a job well done.

The last lesson in the guide is the first step in applying these coaching techniques. We help you start the process the next time you walk into the workplace. You can keep moving yourself and your employees forward every day—building success on success.

"The goal of good coaching isn't just to help employees achieve a certain specific goal. One success engenders another and instills the self-confidence that leads to high levels of performance and productivity in all tasks."

☐ ~~Be a boss!~~

☑ Be a coach

Your job isn't to correct mistakes, find fault, or assess blame. Your job is to achieve productivity goals by coaching your staff to peak performance.

You can do that best by being more of a coach and less of a boss.

A boss talks; a coach listens. A boss tries to fix a problem; a coach keeps problems from happening. A boss gives orders; a coach issues challenges. A boss works on his employees; a coach works with them. A boss passes out blame; a coach takes responsibility.

A good coach is positive, enthusiastic, supportive, trusting, respectful, and patient.

That's not to suggest that you're supposed to be a buddy and a pal. You're still in charge; you're just seeing your charge in a new way.

To lead them, you must serve them, anticipating their needs.

5

Being supportive means a lot more than providing an encouraging word and a pat on the back. As a coach, your job is to get workers what they need to do their jobs well. This includes tools, time, instruction, answers to questions, and protection from outside interference.

Do you trust your employees to be conscientious, to tell the truth, and to give a reasonable day's work for a day's pay?

You'd better. You shouldn't hire them unless you're willing to trust them. Most people are conscientious and honest; they want to do their jobs well. Tell them what to do, and then get out of the way and let them do it.

Respect them. Respect their rights as employees and as human beings. Learn who they are and treat them as individuals.

Here are three keys to being an effective coach for your employees:

Take responsibility: Being trusting and respectful doesn't let you off the hook; managers have to manage. Harry Truman said it best: "The buck stops here."

Be assertive: Seek results, not excuses or reasons. Be a strong presence. Make sure your "yes" means "yes," and your "no" means "no."

Work with your employees, not on them: You're in this thing together, and you share common goals. When they do well, you do well.

"You can choose your attitude—if being a better manager means enough to you. Learn by doing, one trait at a time."

☐ ~~Force them~~

☑ Motivate them

From the biggest go-getter to the person who just seems to be putting in time, the people who work for you are all motivated by three strong forces that get them up in the morning.

1. The need to achieve
2. The burn to learn
3. The craving to contribute

This shouldn't be too big a surprise; these are the same three things that motivate you.

Let's look at each one in turn.

1. **The need to achieve.** To feed that need to achieve, empty praise is just empty calories. Mastery comes from what you can do, not what people say about what you can do. You achieve mastery; nobody can give it to you. Help your

employees master new skills. Keep them striving to reach the next level.

2. **The burn to learn.** If your purpose is to motivate learning, "grading" (or any external evaluation) has never worked and never will. In fact, rewards and punishments often do more harm than good. Beyond paychecks and performance reviews, beyond any external motivation you could ever create, the burn to learn makes learning inevitable—if you create an atmosphere where learning can happen.

3. **The craving to contribute.** Give your employees real work that matters, and give them what they need to get it done. Let them know how their efforts fit into the big picture, especially if their work is only part of the effort going into a large project.

Here are three simple techniques for challenging your employees:

Let them do the job: When you assign them a goal, also assign them the responsibility for doing it and give them the means to do it right.

Match the worker to the task: Plan for success, not failure. Match their skills and aptitudes with the jobs.

Focus on process as well as product: The journey is often as important as the destination. Help employees work through the steps, gaining mastery as they go.

"Put a challenge, the necessary resources, and workers together with a clearly defined goal and stand back. You won't need to teach—but they'll sure learn!"

☐ Make your own
  decisions

☑ **Ask for their
  opinions**

You're the boss; you should make the calls, right?
You're paid to make decisions, and you're responsible for the outcomes. But that doesn't mean you
can't and shouldn't involve the people you work
with in the decision-making process.

"How do you think we should handle it?" can be
one of the most important things you ever say to an
employee.

When you ask for their input, three good things
happen, even before you get an answer.

1. You show your respect for your employee.
2. You show that you don't think you have all the
    answers.

3. You open yourself up to a chance to get valuable information. And that means you can make better decisions.

Asking is only half the process. Listening is the other half. Give employees your full attention. Show them by word and gesture that you're paying attention. Ask questions.

You won't necessarily share their perspectives, but it's important that you try to understand them. And you won't necessarily agree with their solutions, but you should take them seriously and consider them carefully.

It takes courage and initiative for an employee to speak up to the boss. Reward that courage with your words and actions. Questions and suggestions are positive contributions, not threats. They'll make you a better manager.

Here are three tips to help you seek employee input effectively:

Ask for their opinions—and then listen to what they say: They'll assume you don't want their input unless you ask for it. They may not trust you when you do. Be patient and keep asking.

Take their ideas seriously: That doesn't mean you'll agree. But, if they offer the input sincerely, you should take it seriously. If you think an idea's good, say so. If you think it's flawed, say why. Discuss ideas, not personalities.

Check with your employees before making a decision that affects them: When a decision impacts your employees' working conditions or job description, it's doubly important for you to ask before you act. You'll gain their confidence and make better decisions.

"You may be wasting one of your most valuable resources—your employees' good ideas."

☑ Admit your mistakes

"Failure is success if we learn from it."
—Malcolm Forbes

As you can see, that quote comes not from a philosopher, but from a successful businessman, Malcolm Forbes.

The total quality management movement gave us a lot of great ideas, but "zero tolerance for errors" wasn't one of them.

Everyone makes mistakes—including you. Admit them. Fix them. Learn from them. And then move on.

The folks who work with you know you're human. They'll have a lot more confidence in you if you show them you know it, too.

If the notion of making a mistake still bothers you, call it something else. Call it learning.

The story of Thomas Alva Edison and the light bulb is worth retelling in this context. Edison tried hundreds of different materials trying to find a filament that would heat up when an electric current passed through it, giving off light without burning up. After hundreds of disappointments, Edison still had no guarantee that the idea would ever work. And yet he kept trying.

Finally Edison found the magic element—tungsten—and abolished bedtime forever.

When asked how he was able to endure all those failures, Edison reportedly said that he hadn't considered any of his attempts as failures. He was simply learning what wouldn't work.

Mistakes teach us what doesn't work. That's very valuable information.

When you fall short of your goal, learn and go on. You may have to redefine your goal, alter your approach, or get help. But, as long as you continue to try, you can never fail.

Here are the three steps in successfully handling mistakes:

Admit them: Attempts to cover a mistake or to pass the blame for it waste time and energy, engender ill-will, and make the original problem worse. Take the hit.

Fix them: As much as possible, fix any bad feelings or misunderstandings the mistake may have caused.

Learn from them: Is the goal reasonable? Is the approach workable? Is the problem in procedure or execution? Do we need to tinker, press forward, or start over?

"I never get writer's block. When I get stuck, I just lower my standards."

—William Stafford

☐ ~~Protect your privacy~~

☑ Be accessible

Is your door always open?

It shouldn't be.

You need to schedule no-hassle times when you're free to think without interruption. That goes for phone calls, e-mails, and drop-ins. Early morning, before the pace picks up, works best for some folks (if, that is, they tend to be creative and energetic early). Whenever you do it, carve out a creativity session, just you and the muse, several times a week, if not daily.

But, the rest of the time, your employees should feel free to pop in and talk. You can learn more from such informal one-on-one sessions than a dozen structured meetings.

So, you say your door is open, but nobody's walking through it?

A survey by Market Facts' TeleNation indicated that more than 90 percent of the employees polled believe they have good ideas about how their companies could be run more successfully. However, only 38 percent think their employers would be interested in hearing those ideas. The same goes for complaints, only more so.

Unless you let them know you welcome their "interruptions"—and unless you really mean it when you tell them—you won't see much of them, and you'll be a poorer manager because of it.

Just having an open door isn't enough. Get up and get out of the office ("management by wandering around," they call it). Be where they can find and approach you easily.

Here are three suggestions for making those informal encounters profitable:

Listen actively: Of course you're in a hurry to get back to your own work. But, put it aside for a minute and make sure you hear what they're saying.

Ask follow-up questions: If you don't understand a point, say so. Don't bluff so you can appear to be the all-knowing expert on everything.

Accept bad news as well as good: If they think you only want to hear the good stuff, that's all you'll get, at the expense of knowing what's really going on.

"You show that you value an opinion by listening to it, by taking it seriously, and by rewarding it."

☑ Be a good listener

We spend a lot of time in school learning how to "communicate" and "express ourselves."

But who learns how to listen?

Listening is a crucial skill for any manager, especially if you want to manage by coaching.

If you've set up a meeting/conversation ahead of time, be sure to do your homework before your employee arrives. If you need to, check the personnel file, make a phone call or two, anticipate the points you need to cover—whatever it takes to be ready.

When your employee arrives, drop everything and give them your complete attention.

Maintain eye contact. You'll convey your interest and sincerity, and you can also pick up a lot of information about how your employees are feeling and how much they're understanding.

Hear them out before you respond. If you find yourself thinking "I know what you're going to say," you can be pretty sure you don't. Be patient. Stay focused. And resist the temptation to interrupt.

Don't ignore emotions. Acknowledge and verify them. "You sound angry, Ted. Tell me about it."

Allow for silence—but don't use it as a weapon. Silence can be intimidating, but a pause that allows for reflection shows respect and lets your employee give an accurate response, rather than one that's simply fast.

Here are the 3 Rs of effective listening:

Receive: To understand it, you have to hear it. Be still. Wait. Don't assume. Take notes if you need to. Probe gently. Concentrate on what you're hearing (and not on what you have to do or say next).

Reflect: Think about what you're hearing. Make sense out of it. Put it into a meaningful context. Ask questions if you need to. Listening is active!

Rephrase: Bounce what you think you're hearing back to the source. Put it in your own words to make sure you understand it and that you've got it right. Give your employee a chance to clarify.

"Effective listening is simply a means to an end. Once you've heard and understood, you must respond. If you think the employee is wrong, say so. If you don't respond, employees will soon stop talking."

☐ Have all the answers

☑ Ask good questions

Asking good questions is a vital part of effective listening.

So, what's a "good" question? Good question.

A good question is brief, clear, focused, relevant, and constructive. So far, so good. Those five guidelines apply to any type of communication.

But an effective question can be especially tricky, because it should also be neutral and it may need to be open-ended.

Don't confuse "neutral" with "neutered." A good question may be controversial, perhaps even confrontational. But, a good question doesn't imply the "right" answer. Question: "Do you think we should improve the quality of our publication by hiring a freelance editor?"

"Right" answer: Yes! Who wouldn't be in favor of improving quality?

Same question, different phrasing: "Do you think we should add an extra step in the editorial process by hiring a freelance editor?"

"Right" answer: No! Who wants to add extra steps?

Same question, value-neutral: "Do you think we should hire a freelance editor to work on the publication?"

An effective question may also need to be open-ended. If you need more than a simple "yes" or "no," avoid asking "yes" or "no" questions.

You may also need to avoid giving closed choices—like this one:

"Do you think we should hire a freelancer or let Frank do it?"

The answer might be "none of the above," but a subordinate might not feel comfortable turning down both of your alternatives. Try something like this:

"What do you think we ought to do about getting the publication edited?"

Here are three quick keys to asking effective questions:

Give them time to think: As with all forms of effective listening, a little silence can get you a much more thoughtful response. "Why don't you get back to me on that by the end of the week?" might be an appropriate approach at times.

Tell them what's at stake: Does my job depend on my answer? Will I get in trouble if I don't agree with you? Am I venturing an opinion or making a decision? Does it matter what I think?

Then be quiet and listen: Enough said.

"Be clear about your purpose and honest about your motives. Keep your questions on subject and on target. If an answer strays off the point, tactfully refocus."

☐ Stifle gripes

☑Welcome complaints

Nobody likes criticism, and complaints often create problems for you.

Even so, you should welcome complaints and respond to sincere criticism with a sincere "thank you."

But, first, don't assume your employee is there to complain.

If you start the conversation with "What's your beef now?" you immediately put your employee on the defensive.

Suppose he says, "No beef! I just want to talk about my new assignment."

If you still assume the negative, you hear that he doesn't like that new assignment. So you ask, "What's wrong with it?"

Both of you are now on the defensive. Chances of having a productive conversation are slim to none.

Start over.

When he says, "I want to talk about my new assignment," reply, "Sure. What about it?"

Now you're open to a wide range of possibilities. Here are five:

1. "I love it. Thanks!"

   Okay, that's unlikely. But it is possible.

2. "I don't understand it."

   That isn't a knock. It's a request for help. That's what you're there for.

3. "Why'd you give it to me?"

   That may or may not be a complaint. Probe gently to find out.

4. "I don't think I can handle it."

   That's either a complaint or a request for help. Find out which. Is the problem lack of knowledge, time, desire, or confidence? Each case requires different handling.

5. "It stinks!"

   That's a complaint! It might even feel like a slap in the face. But, you're much better off if the employee brings it to you. Don't slap back. Take a deep breath and start asking questions (the coach's best friend).

"What's the problem?" is a good start. Keep probing for specifics until you get the problem defined. Then, you can start to solve it together.

Here are three ways to communicate your willingness to hear their complaints:

Positive body language: Your expression is attentive and your arms are at your sides, rather than folded across your chest like a shield.

Listening: A big part of good body language is a closed mouth. Hear them out before you respond.

Immediate reward: Instead of making them "pay," reward them with your attention and your attempt to solve the problem.

"Complaints make you a better manager. Welcome them and deal with them positively."

☐ ~~Lecture the masses~~

☑ Coach one-on-one

Forget those fiery halftime locker-room speeches (or their business equivalent, the motivational meeting). That's not where the coaching really takes place. You do your most effective teaching and motivating one-on-one, face-to-face, without ever raising your voice.

Keep these three elements of a good coaching session in mind for those one-on-one encounters (whether they're scheduled or spontaneous):

1. **Establish a clear purpose.** If the employee initiates the conversation, let her set the agenda. If it's your call, be clear about what you expect the talk to accomplish.
2. **Establish ground rules.** Make sure you have a common understanding of the time frame. Is this going to take ten minutes or an hour? Also make sure it's clear that you're speaking as man-

ager to employee (not "buddy-buddy" or "off the record").

3. **Keep focused.** If the meeting is happening in your office, don't answer the phone, touch the stack of papers on your desk, look at your computer, or fiddle with the stapler. Give the encounter your full attention.

You'll be tempted. If so, turn off the computer monitor and set all the papers aside. You'll reduce your temptation and also show your respect for and interest in your employee.

Here are three more ideas for making your one-on-one coaching effective:

Define the issue clearly: No mystery here. Just make sure you're both talking about the same thing. If the subject is "office inefficiency," you may think you're talking about getting the mail distributed earlier in the afternoon, and he may think you're attacking his office management skills.

Stick to one issue at a time: You won't get a handle on office management in one conversation. But, you might make some real progress on getting the mail distributed by 1:30 P.M.

Keep it in the present tense: Don't bring up the great system they had where you used to work or the way they did it when Gladys was managing the office. Stay in the here and now.

"When you're coaching one-on-one, whatever you do or say should support your connection with your employee."

☐ Use that big vocabulary

☑ Watch your language

Use words that form bridges, rather than raise barriers.

Whether you're coaching an employee, meeting with the Board of Directors, or talking to the man who scrubs the toilets, straight talk is always the shortest distance between two minds.

Be specific. If you tell an employee you have "concerns" about her "work performance," you haven't told her anything helpful. (You have probably scared her, though.) If she's late too often, say so. Put a number on "too often."

Suppose you begin a conversation with "I have a problem with the way the office is being run."

You may think you've been straightforward and direct. You've certainly let the employee know where you stand. But, consider some of the different things she might have heard:

1. "Somebody's really screwing up around here, and I want you to help me get to the bottom of it."
2. "You're really screwing up around here, and I want it to stop!"
3. "I'm not happy with my performance. Any suggestions on how I might improve?"

If you meant #2, and she starts responding to #3, you're off to a very bad start!

Use simple, common words. Eschew obfuscation. Don't tell your tardy employee that her "onsite punctuality modality leaves something to be desired." Speak English.

Here are three more tips for speaking effectively:

Use the known to explain the unknown: If you're speaking about something complicated or abstract, put it in concrete terms. If your employee's into bowling, comparing a tricky personnel problem to trying to pick up the seven-ten split might work. But, talking about a "suicide squeeze" to a nonbaseball fan won't get you to first base.

Avoid clichés: While we're getting sweaty here, keep away from those tired sports clunkers about playing on a "level playing field" and "fumbling the ball on the goal line." Clichés have lost all their power to evoke an image or even command attention.

Don't use profanity: Never. Not once. I'm not being a prude here. This is the workplace, and you need to set the proper tone. Besides, you never know who you might be offending. Why take a chance?

"How you say it is every bit as important as what you say—sometimes more important."

□ ~~Coach for conformity~~

☑ Celebrate the differences

You can motivate them. You can direct their energies. You can teach them, lead them, and guide them.

But, you can't really control them. You shouldn't try. You shouldn't even want to.

If you want to control employees, you have to watch them all the time. As soon as you're not looking, they may rebel and go back to doing things their way. That requires you to exercise "eternal vigilance"—which is a rotten way to spend the day and it keeps you from doing anything productive.

Don't control: coach for results, giving clear directions and defining the goal. Then, trust them.

When you evaluate their job performance and related workplace behaviors, put your perceptions to this test:

"Is what they're doing wrong or is it just different from the way I'd do it?"

Too many supervisors manage by the "my way or the highway" standard. They view a different approach as a threat to their authority.

You can waste a lot of time and engender a lot of anger and resentment if you make people undo and redo things they did competently the first time.

Part of your job as manager/coach is to learn your workers' individual work styles and allow them to do things their way whenever possible—as long as they get the results you want, when you want them.

The same goes when you're called on to edit their written work. You must, of course, edit for clarity and accuracy. You should help them achieve concision. But, when it comes to idiom and voice—the way an individual "sounds" on paper—let them be them.

Let these three slogans guide you:

If it ain't broke, don't fix it: This sounds simple, but it's worth keeping in the back of your mind when you're tempted to do something untoward.

If it is broke, let them fix it: They'll take ownership and be more motivated because of it.

If they can't fix it, fix it with them: That's an essential part of leadership and teamwork.

"You don't want compliant slaves. You want effective, creative, and competent colleagues."

☐ Make yourself
indispensable

☑ Empower independent employees

"**M**y people won't make a move without asking me first."

Is that you?

If so, you're not doing your job as a manager. You're much too busy trying to do everybody else's job.

You're paid to make decisions, and you're responsible for the outcomes. But, that doesn't mean you can't and shouldn't involve the people you work with in the decision-making process.

"How do you think we should handle it?" can be one of the most important things you ever say to an employee.

But, after you ask, you often need to stand aside and let them carry out the plan.

Maybe you'd like to think the whole company would fall apart if you weren't there, but you can't afford such self-indulgence. Trying to make yourself indispensable is just plain bad management.

Coach workers so well that they become confident enough to carry out plans without you and capable enough to do the job well.

When you let them take the lead, three good things happen.

1. You show your respect for your employee.
2. You show that you don't think you have to do it all.
3. You open yourself up to the possibility that they'll do the job better than you could have.

Your workers are often a lot closer to the problem than you are. They may have a much better sense of how to solve it. Give them a shot. You won't lose face; you'll gain respect.

How do you create an independent workforce? Here are the three primary guidelines:

Hire employees for independence, not subservience: You don't want a good follower. You want a potential leader, someone who makes the calls (and even questions your call at times).

Foster independence: Provide knowledge, information, and, most of all, trust. If you coach your employees well, you won't have to correct them later.

Get out of the way: Give them room to work, to make decisions, and to accept consequences.

"You may be wasting one of your most valuable resources—your employees' talents. The better the manager you are, the less control you need over your workers."

☐ ~~Reserve judgment~~

☑ Make the call

"**N**ot to decide is to decide," a theologian named Harvey Cox once said.

If you fail to make a decision, you decide by default. You also abandon your role as leader and turn the fate of your project over to the prevailing wind or the strongest personality in the group.

Get input, involve your employees in the process from the beginning, and take them with you every step of the way.

But, when it comes time to make the call, there can only be one arbiter, and you're it.

Deciding not to act may be a valid choice. Sometimes doing nothing is the most effective strategy. And empowering one of your employees to make the decision is also perfectly valid. But, failing to decide at all is never a good call. Get as much information and input as you can. Weigh possible courses of action carefully. Then, make the call.

Haste makes waste? Sure, sometimes. But waiting makes nothing, and failing to decide may create a real mess.

Make your decision. Don't look back. If you need to modify your course later, do it. No ship sails across the ocean in a straight line. It makes a series of tacking maneuvers.

If you find yourself hesitant or unwilling to make a decision, these three observations about decision-making can help you.

You don't have to know everything: Good thing, because you never will. Make yourself as well informed as possible; then, make the best decision you can, based on what you know.

You don't have to be sure: Decisions feel a whole lot better when they come with a sense of certainty. But, you can't afford to wait until you're certain. And, remember, sometimes when you're dead-certain, you can still be dead-wrong.

You don't even have to be right: The number-one fear when making a decision is being wrong (especially if you're in a position where your mistakes are quite visible).

"The percentage of mistakes in quick decisions is no greater than in long-drawn-out vacillations, and the effect of decisiveness itself makes things go and creates confidence."

—Anne O'Hare McCormick

☐ Provide ~~all the~~ answers

☑ Solve problems together

Having trouble selling your solutions? Do you have a hard time getting your work force to buy into your plan?

That's because it's your plan, not theirs.

Let your employees in on the initial planning and get their input throughout. You'll come up with a solution everybody can own.

Yeah, it takes longer to get to that solution when you talk about it. Would you rather spend the time creating the solution or scrambling to fix all those "solutions" that didn't work?

If you include employees in the problem-solving process, you get more motivated, confident employees. You also get better solutions.

Here's the process:

- **Define the opportunity.** It's a management cliché, but that doesn't make it wrong: a problem really is a challenge, and a challenge is an opportunity.
- **Define the goal.** Once you have the opportunity, the goal usually becomes obvious. Make sure. Put it into words everyone understands and agrees with.
- **Define the actions you need to take.** Once you have a clearly defined goal, laying out the steps needed to get there becomes much more manageable.
- **Create the plan.** Who's going to do what? And, when are they going to have it done? The most important element in any plan is the next step. What do we do next?
- **Create the evaluation standard.** How will we know when we've arrived?
- **Confirm understanding.** Before you end a planning session, make sure everyone has the same notions of what you've decided. Repeat and paraphrase key points and put it in writing for everyone to review.
- **Plan the follow-up.** Make sure everyone knows what they are supposed to do next, and then set a deadline for a progress report.

Your discussions should be as free and open as you can make them. Here are three ways to accomplish this:

Create as many possibilities as you can for input before you start focusing on a single solution: This gives you a pool of ideas to choose from.

Separate the idea from the person who proposed it: You want to discuss plans, not personalities.

If an idea is offered sincerely, take it seriously: Nothing kills creative problem-solving faster than ridicule.

"Resist the temptation to assign the person who came up with the suggestion the task of carrying it out. You want to encourage innovation, remember?"

☐ Don't be the bad guy

☑ Deliver the bad news personally

If you're like most managers, you probably hate being the bearer of bad tidings.

We all want people to like us, and we aren't very likeable when we're telling folks things they don't want to hear, such as:

- You don't get a merit raise this year.
- Your project didn't get funded.
- You're going to have to increase productivity by 15 percent—with no increase in budget or personnel, and, that all-time favorite,
- Your services won't be needed after June 30th (or any other variation on "You're fired!").

Bad news is inevitable. You could dodge the responsibility of delivering it yourself, but if you do, you'll probably make matters worse, and you'll earn

61

a reputation for being evasive and even cowardly as a manager.

Rather than ducking this hard duty, you need to develop strategies for handling it effectively.

Come directly to the point. A little small talk may help relax both of you, but the longer you delay, the more tension you create. Your employee knows you didn't call him in to talk about the weather.

Select an appropriate time and place. The setting may be as important as the message. Make sure you have privacy and you won't be interrupted.

Don't invite your employee to sit, and then remain standing (elevating yourself while diminishing him). Don't sit on a "throne" (a better, higher, bigger chair). And don't retreat behind your desk or any other barrier.

Above all, minimize the confrontational aspect of the conversation by following these three guidelines:

Offer reasons: It isn't so just because you say it's so. You need to explain why you've reached the conclusion that an employee's performance is subpar or that their behavior is inappropriate. Explain the "why" as you deliver the "what."

Speak to actions, not motives: You're a coach, not a therapist. You're coaching performance, not personality. Limit your message to what they do, not who they are or why they do it.

Offer options: If the news is anything short of termination, tell the employee what they can do to improve the situation. Don't end the session until you both are clear on what the employee should do next.

"How will your comments help them do their jobs better? How will that improved performance help them grow and advance?"

☐ Don't get mad

☑ Don't act out of anger

"**D**on't get mad; get even," the old axiom advises. But, there's an even better way—don't do either.

A worker makes a mistake, and you lash out, administering a loud public reprimand. It's only natural. You're righteously mad. All your hard work has been wasted in one stupid, careless moment. You gave the worker thorough instructions, and he fouled things up anyway. He had the tongue-lashing coming.

Besides, if you try to bottle up your anger, you're courting a heart attack or a stroke. Let it all out. Vent that spleen. You'll feel better. Right?

Wrong. Dead wrong.

By acting on anger, you hurt your relationship with your employee—and everyone within earshot—and actually endanger your own health.

The battered worker has learned only one thing—that you're a blowhard. Now he's angry, too, and embarrassed and ashamed.

Everybody within earshot has also learned the same lesson: you can't control your anger. They'll all walk on tiptoe in your presence, working to avoid mistakes and evade blame, rather than working to solve problems and produce results.

And, by venting your anger, you're actually feeding it, becoming more angry for a longer time. You're also compounding the harm to your body and psyche by prolonging the physiological responses (adrenaline surge, rapid heartbeat, elevated blood pressure).

You can't undo the mistake. If you let it provoke you to act in anger, you're probably going to make it worse.

Feeling anger—along with frustration and disappointment—is natural. But, you don't have to let the feeling control your actions.

Here are three steps that can enable you to ride out the adrenaline rush:

Calm yourself: Take a few deep breaths. Relax your shoulders. Talk yourself down. (Counting to ten really does help you diffuse your anger.)

Remove yourself: If you can't handle the situation yet, walk away until you can.

Do the right thing: Instead of doing the "natural thing" by blowing up, try to do the right thing and think before you act.

"Anger, if not restrained, is frequently more harmful than the wrong that provoked it."
                                                    —Seneca

☐ Put it in writing

☑ Avoid memo mania

When computers first entered the workplace, we were supposed to reap two huge benefits.

First, we were supposed to enter the "golden age of leisure." With computers making work so much easier and faster, we'd free up days, even weeks, of free time.

That didn't happen. We just upped our expectations of how much work we should do and how fast we should do it.

Computers were also supposed to usher in the paperless office. Everything would be on-screen, on disk, and online.

That didn't happen either. In fact, computers generate more paper, and your workers may be drowning in it.

Are you sure you need to put it in writing? And, if you do, are you sure your employees have to read it—or even touch it? And, will what you say help them improve?

Paper takes time—to handle, to read, and to dispose of. It also takes up space and creates clutter. If you can eliminate unnecessary paper, you've done your workers and yourself a big favor.

Don't misunderstand. Failing to put an agreement or a decision in writing because you don't want to be held responsible for it is dishonest and evasive. Many communications must be given permanent form for future reference.

But, you may be using memos to avoid personal contact with employees—with their messy questions and objections.

There's another potential danger with the written memo: once you write and circulate it, you may make the mistake of assuming all your employees received, read, and understood it. Unless the communication calls for a specific response, you have no way of knowing what happened to it on the receiving end.

Here are three ways you can eliminate unnecessary paper:

E-mail it: Electronic mail creates its own clutter and can be just as anonymous as paper. But it may be more appropriate and less cumbersome for many messages.

Post it: Most offices now have an electronic bulletin board, a cyber repository for reports. Let folks know how they can access material if they need it, making it easy for them to avoid it if they don't.

Forget it: Best of all, if you really examine the message, you may discover it's redundant, irrelevant, or just plain ridiculous.

"Make sure the message is worth the ink, the paper, and your employees' precious time."

☐ ~~Abolish meetings~~

☑ Manage meetings

People don't hate meetings.

We say we do. We grouse about having to go to them (unless we called the meeting, and sometimes even then). But, in fact, meetings are important, and most folks know it, at least on some level. As a coach and manager, it's up to you to make sure meetings serve the purposes for which they are called. For example,

- Meetings provide a social component in a workplace where employees are increasingly isolated, in their cubicles, at their computers.
- Meetings ensure everyone hears the same thing at the same time, a much-more reliable way to communicate than via that notorious grapevine.
- Most important, meetings allow for interaction—questions, clarifications, discussion, an opportunity to solve problems and reach a consensus.

No, it isn't meetings folks hate; they hate bad meetings.

They hate being subjected to nonsense. They hate wasting their time. They hate listening to someone read a list of announcements to them, when they could have read them (selectively, skipping what didn't apply to them) much faster for themselves.

And employees really loathe spending their precious time discussing an issue that matters to them, only to find out that a decision has already been made.

Run your meetings tightly. An effective agenda includes not only the topics for discussion, but also the time allotted for each discussion. Keep the discussion moving, making sure to recognize employees who are less aggressive about getting their opinions in. If you aren't the best person to run the meeting, delegate that responsibility to the one who is.

When planning that meeting, keep these three guidelines in mind:

Hold meetings only when necessary: If you merely need to announce information, perhaps a memo, an e-mail, or a web site post will do. Save meetings for meaningful interactions.

Plan every meeting carefully: Don't plan only the topics to cover and the best order to cover them in, but also the environment you want for the discussion.

Circulate discussion items and necessary information ahead of time: Let workers know what's expected of them at the meeting. ("Please read this over and come with your comments.")

"Get them out on time. If you promised an hour, keep it to an hour."

☐ ~~Expect them to know~~

☑ Train them

Hire for aptitude and attitude. Train for knowledge.

To be an effective trainer, you must first master the task. If you can't do it, you can't teach it, either.

But, that doesn't mean you have to know everything—or pretend you do. Too many managers try to hide their massive ignorance behind their slender knowledge. It's like trying to hide an elephant behind a palm tree.

Employees figure out soon enough if you don't know what you're doing. You're much better off letting them know you know it, too—and that you're willing to learn. Be open about your ignorance; just don't stay in it. Get training yourself. Read, observe, and ask questions. Do your homework.

When you're ready to tackle a training session, follow these simple steps:

1. **Prepare to present.** Think through the process. Break it down into simple steps. Approach it from the point of view of someone new to the task. Jot key steps on a 3×5 notecard. (If you can't fit the information on a 3×5 card, you haven't made it simple enough.)

2. **Rehearse.** No matter how well you think you know the process, you need to practice explaining it. Mentally go through the steps several times.

3. **Prepare to demonstrate.** Work through the process several times. If possible, work on the same equipment your employees will be using when you train them. Then, you'll be ready to show while you tell; your presentation will be much more effective.

4. **Apply the KYHO principle.** That stands for Keep Your Hands Off. After you demonstrate the process, step aside and let your employees do it. Answer questions. Give prompts. But, keep your hands clasped firmly behind your back.

Here are three bonus tips for being an effective trainer:

Remove the distractions: If possible, get everybody away from phones, beepers, and pagers (including your own).

Respect their intelligence: Your employees may be ignorant about the process, but assume they're as smart as you are. Don't talk down.

Build on what they know: The voice mail system may be new, but they know what a telephone is. Find out where they are and take them to the next step.

"They haven't learned it until they can do it without you."

☐ ~~Give 'em hell~~

☑ **Stress the positive**

Accentuate the positive with your employees—but not because you think it will make them like you. You're not there to be a buddy. Be positive because it will make you a more effective manager.

Consider the way you ask your employees questions—this is a key skill in seeking their input on decision making.

Attendance at your weekly staff meetings (supposedly mandatory) has been lousy. You decide to seek advice from one of the loyal employees who has been showing up for every session. Here's one way to ask:

"What should we do to punish people who don't come to meetings?"

You've narrowed all the possible responses you might have gotten to one—a negative one: punishments. Your employee might have something else to suggest, but she may not do so now.

Another approach:

"How can we get people to stop skipping the meetings?"

That's better. You've opened the question to include any sort of answer the employee might want to give you. But you're still using negative language ("stop" and "skipping").

Here are two ways to translate the question into positive terms:

- "How can we get more people to attend meetings?"
- "How can we make the meetings better, so everyone will want to show up?"

It's more than just a matter of phrasing. These are completely different questions, and they'll get different—better—answers.

Admittedly, discussing the negative question could be more fun, but discussing the positive can be more productive and may lead you to solutions.

Maybe the question you really want to ask is:

"Do we really need those stupid meetings?"

If so, put it in the positive. That means more than just cutting out the "stupid." Ask in a way that can yield helpful information, perhaps starting with:

"What's the function of the weekly meeting?"

Here are the three keys to keeping things positive:

Avoid inflated adverbs: Words like "always" and "never" increase the emotional content of any statement. "You're always late" or "you're never on time" are probably overstatements.

Don't resort to euphemisms: "Let's take a look at your punctuality issues" isn't more positive; it's just evasive.

Stress desired outcomes: Stay away from historical grievances and the blame game. Look forward.

"Whatever you say, say it clearly and simply—and put it in the positive."

☐ Money talks

☑ Reward what you want

It sounds so simple, and yet many managers fail to follow this basic principle. Too often, managers ignore competence and focus only on subpar performance or unacceptable behavior.

Encourage peak performance by rewarding it.

A pay increase and advancement in rank are the biggest and most tangible rewards, but they're not the only ones. Other effective rewards include time off (from a few hours to a sabbatical) and perks (a reserved parking space, more flexible hours, an office with a window, and box seats to a local sports venue, to name a few).

The tangible reward may be purely symbolic—of no real monetary value—but an "Employee of the Month" plaque and a profile in the company newsletter may have great symbolic value.

And don't underestimate the value of intangible rewards.

Most employees assume money is the primary positive motivator in the workplace. But, surveys of worker attitudes put money in fourth or fifth place on the list of motivators. Intangibles like "job satisfaction," "chances to learn," and "independence" consistently take the top spots.

Reward workers by trusting them. Give them greater control over their work lives and allow for increased responsibility—so long as you tie it to the authority and the resources they need in the new role.

Provide chances for your employees to increase mastery and skill, to learn and grow, and to take ownership of and pride in their work. They'll work hard for the rewards inherent in the performance itself. Give them means and opportunity. They'll do the rest.

Here are three rules of rewarding:

Link rewards to behaviors: The reward will reinforce the action only if it comes as a consequence of that action—and the employee knows it. It can be as simple as, "Exceed your sales goal and get your bonus."

Confer rewards fairly: This is no place to pay off friends or favor pets. Set objective performance standards and reward accordingly.

Make sure everybody understands the rules: Communicate performance criteria clearly. Announce rewards publicly. Avoid the appearance, as well as the reality, of favoritism.

"A 'fair' system of rewards doesn't mean that the rewards will even out over time. All workers must have an equal opportunity to compete for the reward, but the rewards must go to those who earn them."

☐ Don't overpraise

☑ Provide positive feedback

What if someone very significant in your life, someone with the power to affect your mood and determine your future, gave you feedback on your performance only once a year, and then only on a generic evaluation form? Ridiculous, right?

And, yet, many employees work hard, day in and day out, without any meaningful feedback other than the annual performance review, which is often only a perfunctory exercise in paper shuffling.

Are you giving your employees regular, meaningful feedback on their work? If not, you're missing one of the greatest coaching opportunities and a great chance to improve employee performance.

Most of us don't miss a chance to chew our employees out and correct their errors. That seems to come naturally, and we accept it as part of our jobs as managers. But, what about the positive feedback for a job well done, praise for hitting or exceeding the mark?

For too many workers, feedback means criticism. But, constant criticism is seldom effective in coaching workers to peak performance. In fact, negative feedback can actually suppress performance, as workers hide their mistakes and avoid taking chances.

Feedback must include praise for work well done and for honest effort that fails to yield results through no fault of the worker.

To be effective, feedback must be timely. The further the comment becomes separated from the deed, the less emotional impact it has. (That's one reason why the annual review is such an empty exercise.)

Also follow these three hallmarks of effective positive feedback:

Recognize individuals: Employees take pride in playing on an effective team and sharing in the reflected glory of a team victory. But, that doesn't mean they don't appreciate being singled out for their contributions.

Offer specific examples: The general "nice work" isn't nearly as effective as specific praise for specific behavior. "I thought you did a great job of handling the discussion. Your patience and your willingness to hear all points of view were outstanding."

Be sincere: Empty praise is worse than no praise at all. Sincerity is equal parts speaking the truth and speaking it honestly. Your feedback must be genuine, and you must deliver it in a way that is natural and comfortable for you.

"If possible, walk around the workplace regularly, providing feedback—especially positive feedback—whenever appropriate."

☐ Don't be just a cheerleader

☑ Advocate for your employees

Are you willing to go to bat for your employees, to fight for them, to defend them from unjust attacks, and to take your fair share of the blame when something goes wrong?

You really are like a coach. Coaches run practices, teach, make out the lineup, plan strategy, and call the plays. You do those things, too—training, assigning work, giving feedback, evaluating performance.

The good coach, at times, argues with the officials on behalf of the players. You may need to do that, too, bringing injustices to the attention of the bosses to get your staff the recognition they deserve and the materials they need to do their jobs.

This takes guts. It's a lot easier to chew out your subordinates and curry favor with your superiors. But, in this case, the harder way is the right way.

Most good coaches perform one more important function; they root, root, root for the home team—loudly, passionately, and publicly. Coaches are their players' most vocal critics, but they're also their biggest cheerleaders.

That's you, coach—the best cheerleader your players will ever have. Share their triumphs and concerns. Exhort them to peak performance. Reward them with your praise. Savor their achievements with them without taking any of the credit away from them.

They may never thank you for it. They may not even notice. Your reward will be their good performance, and their longevity and loyalty to the job. And, remember, when they look good, you look good.

Keep these three keys in mind when advocating for your employees:

Don't take the credit: We've all seen too many press conferences and awards ceremonies where the boss steps into the spotlight and takes all the bows. That's only fair if the boss did all the work. Bring the folks who did the sweating up on stage.

Don't deflect the blame: If it happens on your watch, it's your responsibility. Take the hit in public, and instruct the employee who made the mistake in private.

Make your employees look good: When you do, they make you look good. And you earn their trust and loyalty.

"Would your workers say you're a 'stand-up boss'? There's no higher praise they could give you."

 □ Start right

☑ Just get started

It doesn't matter where you start.

It only matters that you start.

Action often must come before understanding and almost always comes before certainty.

Don't wait to be inspired. Don't wait for insight. Don't wait until you feel in the mood. Don't wait, period. Start anywhere. You'll work your way toward inspiration and insight.

We tend to put off tasks for one of three reasons:

1. We don't have enough information.
2. We don't feel confident.
3. We just flat out don't want to do it, not now, not ever. (The medical term for this disease is "Lackawanna.")

Most of us would much rather tackle the simple, familiar stuff than the new and potentially difficult.

If you need information, seek it out right now. But be careful. Seeking more info can be a great way to stall. There's always something more you could learn, right?

If you had to feel confident and comfortable before you took on a new task, you'd never learn to ride a bike, let alone drive a car. If you don't feel confident, act as if you do. Confidence comes with mastery, not before.

Face your "Lackawanna" straight on. That's why they call it work, and that's why they pay you to do it, right? You'll feel a whole lot better—and be a whole lot more efficient—if you get the Lackawanna jobs out of the way. Lackawanna happens to managers and employees. One of the goals of the manager who's also a coach is both preventing this malady and/or curing it if it has spread to your group.

Get your employees involved in the process from the beginning, helping you define the problem, develop the approach, and create the plan. It's much better to start off together than to try to bring people in later. You'll wind up saving time from the messes you don't have to clean up and the explanations you don't have to make later.

If you're having trouble getting started, here are three tips:

Don't overanalyze: Try things out. Let ideas flow.

Don't overevaluate: The time for criticism comes after you have something to criticize. Start troubleshooting too soon, and the whole process grinds to a halt.

Don't stop: You're only stuck if you refuse to move.

"Do something. Try something new. Keep learning. It will keep you and your employees enthusiastic."

The McGraw-Hill Mighty Managers Handbooks

The Powell Principles

by Oren Harari (0-07-144490-4)

Details two dozen mission- and people-based leadership skills that have guided Colin Powell through his nearly half-century of service to the United States.

Provides a straight-to-the-point guide that any leader in any arena can follow for unmitigated success.

How Buffett Does It

by James Pardoe (0-07-144912-4)

Expands on 24 primary ideas Warren Buffett has followed from day one.

Reveals Buffett's stubborn adherence to the time-honored fundamentals of value investing.

The Lombardi Rules

by Vince Lombardi, Jr. (0-07-144489-0)

Presents more than two dozen of the tenets and guidelines Lombardi used to drive him and those around him to unprecedented levels of success.

Packed with proven insights and techniques that are especially valuable in today's turbulent business world.

The Welch Way

by Jeffrey A. Krames (0-07-142953-0)

> Draws on the career of Jack Welch to explain how workers can follow his proven model.

> Shows how to reach new heights in today's wide-open, idea-driven workplace.

The Ghosn Factor

by Miguel Rivas-Micoud (0-07-148595-3)

> Examines the life, works, and words of Carlos Ghosn, CEO of *Nissan* and *Renault*.

> Provides 24 succinct lessons that managers can immediately apply.

How to Motivate Every Employee

by Anne Bruce (0-07-146330-5)

> Provides strategies for infusing your employees with a passion for the work they do.

> Packed with techniques, tips, and suggestions that are proven to motivate in all industries and environments.

The New Manager's Handbook

by Morey Stettner (0-07-146332-1)

> Gives tips for teaming with your employees to achieve extraordinary goals.

> Outlines field-proven techniques to succeed and win the respect of both your employees and your supervisors.

The Sales Success Handbook

by Linda Richardson (0-07-146331-3)

Shows how to sell customers—not by what you tell them, but by how well you listen to what they have to say.

Explains how to persuasively position the value you bring to meet the customer's business needs.

How to Plan and Execute Strategy

by Wallace Stettinius, D. Robley Wood, Jr., Jacqueline L. Doyle, and John L. Colley, Jr. (0-07-148437-X)

Provides 24 practical steps for devising, implementing, and managing market-defining, growth-driving strategies.

Outlines a field-proven framework that can be followed to strengthen your company's competitive edge.

How to Manage Performance

by Robert Bacal (0-07-148439-8)

Provides goal-focused, common-sense techniques to stimulate employee productivity in any environment.

Details how to align employee goals and set performance incentives.

Managing in Times of Change

by Michael D. Maginn (0-07-148436-1)

Helps you to understand and explain the benefits of change, while flourishing within the new environment.

Provides straight talk and actionable advice for teams, managers, and individuals.